Which Animals Will We See?

by Megan Litwin

Scott Foresman
is an imprint of

PEARSON

Glenview, Illinois • Boston, Massachusetts • Chandler, Arizona
Upper Saddle River, New Jersey

Every effort has been made to secure permission and provide appropriate credit for photographic material. The publisher deeply regrets any omission and pledges to correct errors called to its attention in subsequent editions.

Unless otherwise acknowledged, all photographs are the property of Scott Foresman, a division of Pearson Education.

Photo locators denoted as follows: Top (T), Center (C), Bottom (B), Left (L), Right (R), Background (Bkgd)

Opener Getty Images; 1 Digital Vision; 3 Getty Images; 4 Brand X Pictures; 5 Getty Images; 6 (B) © Kim Taylor/DK Images, 6 (T) Getty Images; 7 (BL) Getty Images, 7 (T) Digital Vision, 7 (C) Digital Vision; 8 DK Images

ISBN 13: 978-0-328-50712-2
ISBN 10:   0-328-50712-1

We hike into the woods.

Many animals live here.

Which animals will we see?

We can see birds.

They live in a nest.

They are at home in the woods.

We can see a fox.

It can hunt in the snow.

It is at home in the woods.

We can see an ant.

It looks for its nest.

It is at home in the woods.

What a good hike in the woods!
We saw many animals at home
in the woods.
You can see them too!

Ants

As we saw in the book, many different animals make their homes in the woods. Ants are one kind of woods animal. Ants live in nests that have many rooms and tunnels. The nests have one or more queen ants and lots of worker ants. The queen ant is the mother of all the ants in the nest. The worker ants take care of ant eggs and feed baby ants.

8